THIS JOURNAL
holds the wisdom of:

_____

_____

Experience is the great teacher.

You will always leave something behind:
your influence.

A friend is like a rainbow, always there for
you after a storm.

If you aim at nothing, you're bound to hit it.

A handful of patience is worth more
than a bushel of brains.

The dearest things of life are mostly
near at hand.

You begin to slip when you'd rather win an
argument than be right.

Advice is like cooking—you should try it
before you feed it to others.

It is better to hold out a helping hand
than to point a finger.

Advice when most needed is least heeded.

An ounce of work is worth a ton of wishing.

Anyone who practices what he preaches
doesn't have to preach much.

Don't call the world dirty because you've forgotten to clean your windows.

A word to the wise is unnecessary.

Be what you wish others to become.

You can't make cider without apples.

If you don't give up, you haven't lost.

Money is only a tool, not a goal.

Being human is a privilege, not an excuse.

The less we know, the longer it takes
to explain.

Beware of the man who knows the answer
before he understands the question.

Deal with the faults of others as gently
as you do your own.

A man is happier to be sometimes cheated
than to never trust.

Throw mud and you will have dirty hands,
whether the mud hits the mark or not.

Every man must live with the man
he makes of himself.

Good intentions spoil if not used.

Half done is far from done.

Harvest comes not every day.

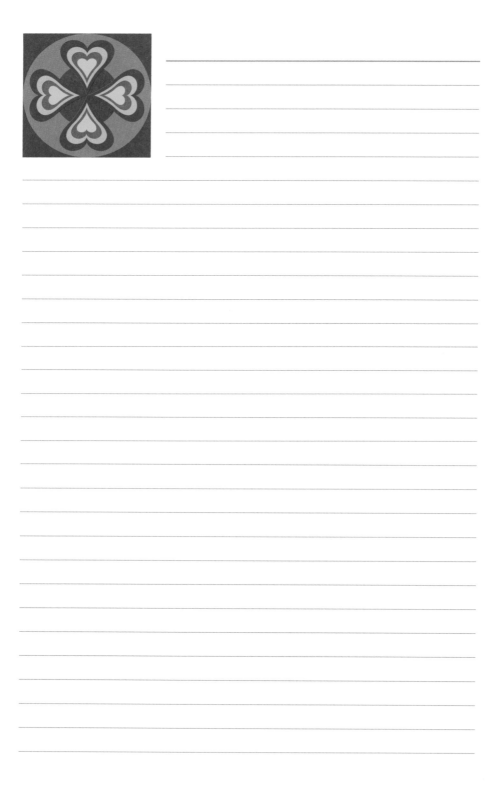

If you must doubt, doubt your doubts,
not your beliefs.

The best way to succeed in life is to act on
the advice you give others.

It is a wealthy person, indeed, who
calculates riches not in gold but in friends.

Don't count your eggs before they are laid.

It is better to suffer wrong than to
commit wrong.

Judge a man by his questions,
not by his answers.

You cannot do everything at once, but you
can do something at once.

If you want a place in the sun, you will have
to expect some blisters.

A great deal of what we see depends
on what we are looking for.

Kindness, when given away,
keeps coming back.

Learning is far more valuable
than education.

Live each short hour with God, and the
long years will take care of themselves.

The more you know, the more you
know you don't know.

Lying in bed dreaming never
got the work done.

Money talks, but it doesn't say when
it's coming back.

A narrow mind and a wide mouth
usually go together.

No joy is complete unless it is shared.

Peace is seeing a sunset and knowing
who to thank.

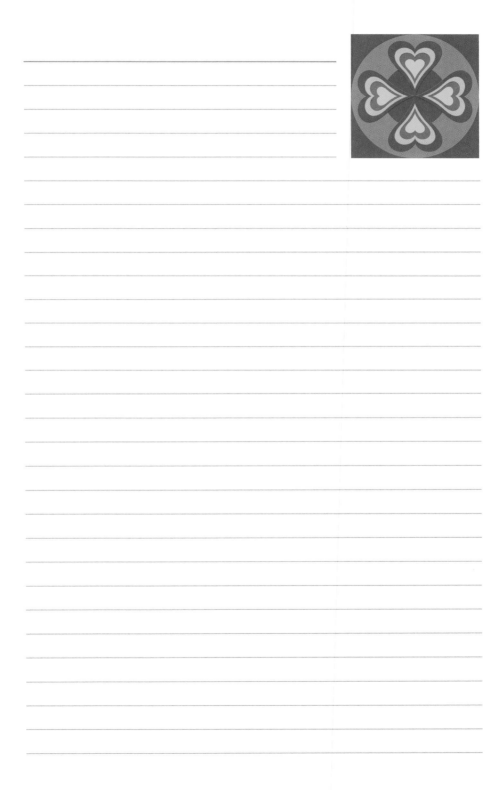

Take all you want; eat all you take.

Teaching children to count is fine, but
teaching them what counts is better.

You can't make good hay from poor grass.

A person who gets all wrapped up in himself
makes a mighty small package.

It takes both rain and sunshine to make
the garden grow.

The time to make friends is before
you need them.

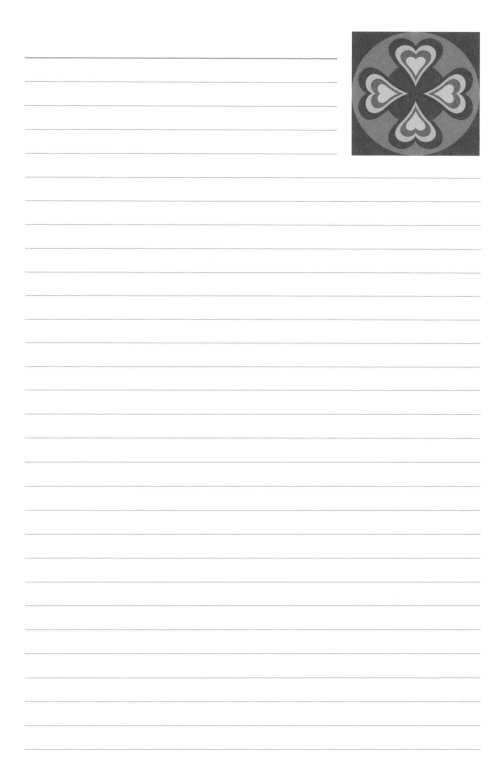

There's a difference between good, sound
reasons and reasons that sound good.

Don't pull up your garden to see
if it's growing.

Those who have no children know best
how to raise them.

You only live once, but if you work it right,
once is enough.

Blunt remarks, like dull knives, often inflict
the severest wounds.

A task takes as long as it takes.

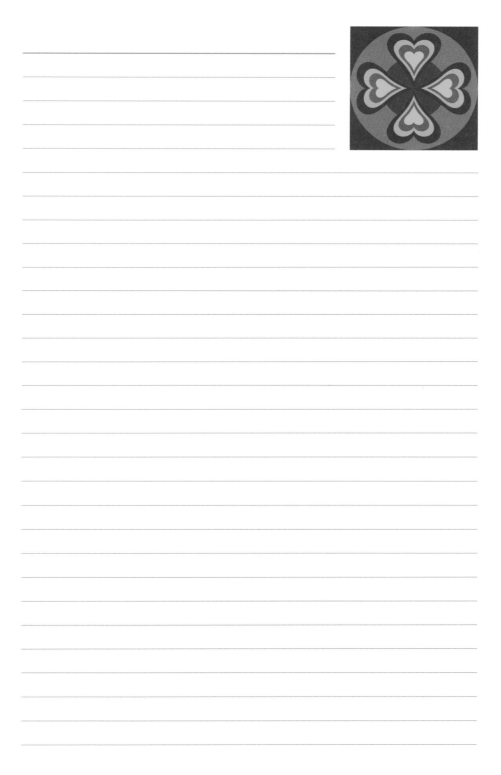

The time to relax is when you don't
have time for it.

To grow old gracefully, you must start when
you are young.

The person who kills time has not learned
the value of life.

A man is never old until his regrets
outnumber his dreams.

To stay youthful, stay useful.

If you're careful of your pennies, the dollars
will take care of themselves.

We don't realize how wonderful today
is until tomorrow.

We need old friends to help us grow old and
new friends to help us stay young.

Things that steal our time are usually
the easiest to do.

What other people think of you is none
of your business.

A pulling horse cannot kick.

Worse than failure is the failure to try.

Good deeds have echoes.

ISBN 978-1-64178-027-8

© 2018 by Quiet Fox Designs, *www.QuietFoxDesigns.com*, an imprint of Fox Chapel Publishing
Company, Inc., 903 Square Street, Mount Joy, PA 17552.

Shutterstock credits: A. L. Spangler (130); Bob Pool (34); Christian Kieffer (114); Dan Thornberg
(66); Delmas Lehman (98); Denise Kappa (82); Derek Gordon (2); Michael G McKinne (18); steven r.
Hendricks (front cover & 50); Vladislav Gajic (144)
Patterns on back cover and endpapers: Justin Speers

We are always looking for talented authors and artists. To submit an idea, please send a brief inquiry to
acquisitions@foxchapelpublishing.com.

Fox Chapel Publishing makes every effort to use environmentally friendly paper for printing.

Printed in China

First printing